IN THE BEGINNING . . .

by Robert Stephen

illustrated by
Robert Ward

AULTON PRESS

First published in 1991 *by*
AULTON PRESS
Ardallie, Peterhead,
Scotland AB42 8BP

British Library Cataloguing in Publication Data
Stephen, Robert, 1949 —

British Library Cataloguing in Publication Data
Stephen, Robert *1949–*
In the beginning.
1. English poetry
I. Title
821.914

ISBN 0 – 9512459 – 2 – 9

Designed & Produced by Aulton Press
Typeset in Baskerville & printed by
M & A Thomson Litho Ltd., Glasgow
Printed on Consort Royal Silk Tint 150gsm, manufactured by
The Donside Paper Company Ltd., Aberdeen

for Robert and Muriel

ACKNOWLEDGEMENTS

I should like to thank Rob Ward, my Pre-Raphaelite illustrator, for his dedication, vision and beautiful paintings, and Elizabeth my wife, publisher and valued adviser for her support and encouragement.

CONTENTS

Old Testament Tales

Psalms, Prayers and Promises

PLATES

APPENDICES

THE RT HON. SIR DAVID STEEL KBE MP

HOUSE OF COMMONS
LONDON SW1A 0AA

FOREWORD

In an age when so many of our youngsters are brought up on a diet of television soap operas and the soulless mechanical language of the computer age, I believe it is essential that we entice them to pay some attention to the old Scots dialect. I can think of few more effective enticements than this truly enchanting work, "In the Beginning . . .". Not, of course, that it is a children's book — it has an enduring appeal to all ages because of its foundation on the more familiar passages of the Old Testament.

Some of the purists may quarrel with parts of the poetry, or its emphasis on the particular dialect of the North East, but I believe that the contribution of Robert Stephen's translation and interpretation of the biblical passages, and Robert Ward's powerful and attractive illustrations will give delight to many. I especially enjoyed the flashes of Scots humour in the story of Noah's Ark and in the description of the boy David preparing to fight Goliath:

Syne David tried the armour on
And clanked aroon a while.
"I canna fecht like this", he said:
"The weicht will cramp my style."

Nothing has cramped this successful style and I commend the book warmly.

David Steel

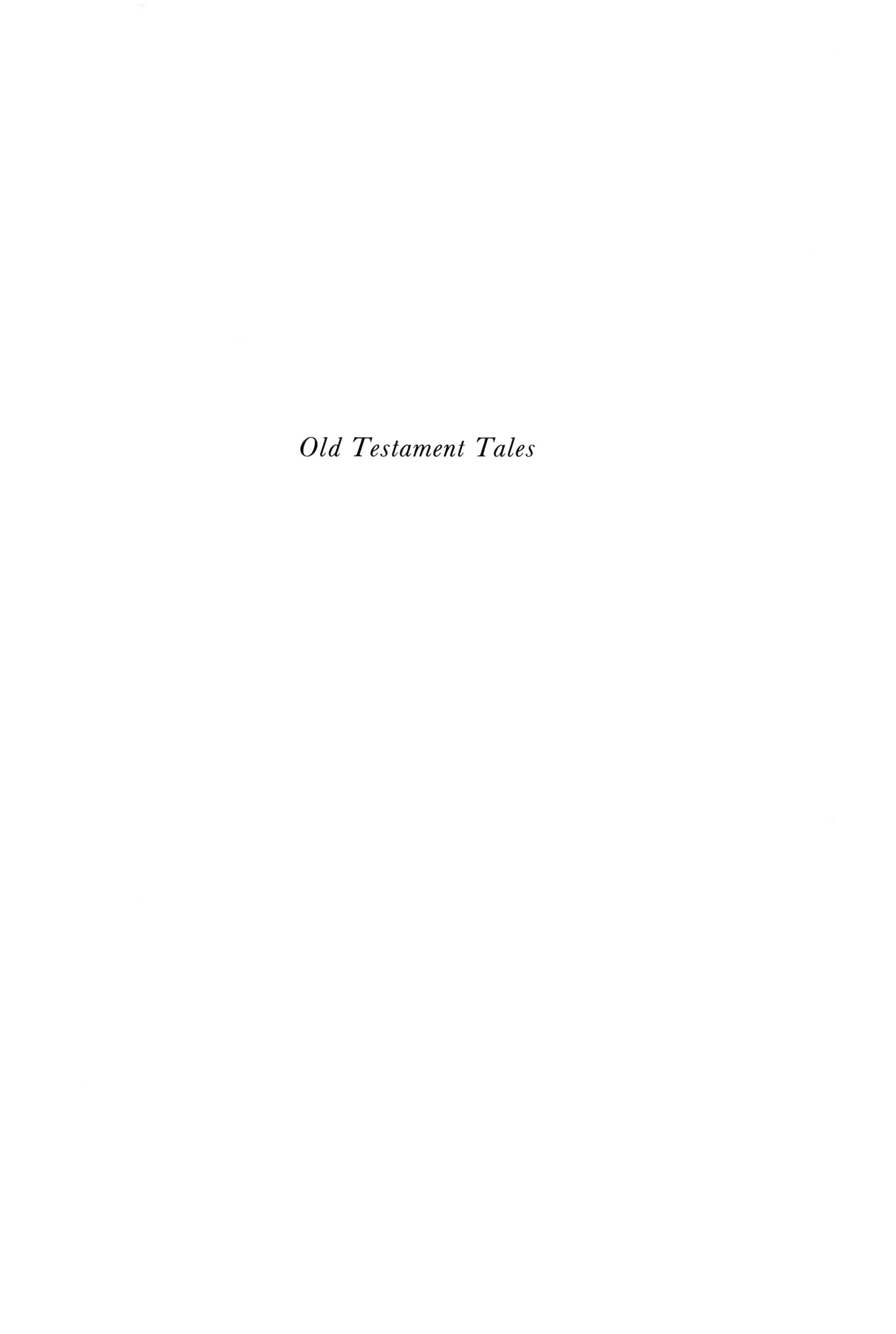

Old Testament Tales

In the Beginning ...

Ere Time began and aa was dark,
Lang ere the world was made,
And Chaos reigned owre the abyss,
"Let there be licht," he said.

And licht there was; he ca'd it *Day*,
And darkness ca'd he *Nicht.*
There was evenin, there was mornin,
And the colours pleased his sicht.

And syne he raised the lift abeen,
Cerulean-tinted dome.
There was evenin, there was mornin,
And the second day had come.

Then he gaithered aa the watters
And he made the seven seas;
And the land he raised abeen them
Whar he planted grass and trees,

And the mony-tinted flooers
And the herbs that sweetly blaw;
Tree and leaf and seed and berry;
Aye, he made them, ane and aa.

Sun, moon and stars he lifted up,
Splendent celestial spheres,
To licht the earth and mark the days
And seasons, signs and years.

Then he filled the teemin watters
Wi fish and muckle whaals,
And every livin craitur
That loups or sweems or crawls

In the oceans. And abeen them,
In the currents o' the air,
He made the tribes o' feathered folk
That ply their business there.

He made aa the little craiturs
That creep upon the grun;
Ox, lion, moose and elephant;
He made them, every one.

He filled the watters, earth and air
Wi rowth o' livin things:
The whaal that blaws, the bull that roars,
The little bird that sings.

And man he made, and woman,
In the mornin world to dwell,
To rule owre his Creation
In the likeness o' himsel.

And seeds and fruits he gave to them
For sustenance and maet,
And to every livin craitur
The herbs that he could aet.

God sat him doon and lookit roon
At a'thing that he'd done.
There was evenin, there was mornin,
And the seventh day had come.

He lookit owre the bonny world,
Owre mountain, plain and flood;
Owre islands, seas and continents,
And he saw that it was good.

And on the seventh day God rested.

Eastward in Eden

And God created Adam
Fae the dust o' the grun
As a potter moulds his clay,
Primeval, first, alone.

And he planted a gairden
Wi blooms sweet and rare
Owre Eastward in Eden.
Nae thorn-tree grew there,

But aa that was bonny
And aa that was good.
In the hert o' the gairden
The tree o' life stood.

And beneath it sprang flooers
Wha's bloom never fades,
Unblemished, undyin,
Like stars in its shade,

Their colours like rainbows
Star-spangled wi dew,
Their fragrance like incense,
Their green ever-new.

And a bit further ower,
Awa by itsel,
Stood the tree o' the knowledge
Of good and of ill.

And up through its branches
Aa glistenin wi dew,
Its tendrils like serpents,
The passion-flower grew.

And aa through the gairden
Sprang trees that were good:
The fig-tree, the olive,
The sweet sandalwood;

And the clusters o' grapes
Hangin thick on the vine,
And the sweet-scented myrrh
In the mornin o' time.

And the birds on the branches
Sang bonny and true
For the joy o' their herts
When a'thing was new.

The lintie, the mavis,
The robin, the lark,
They twittered their gladness
Fae daylicht till dark.

And the river o' Eden
That wattered the sod
Flowed oot through the gairden
Fae the Fountains o' God.

And into this gairden
Whar blooms never fade
The Lord God pit Adam,
The man that he'd made.

And the Lord spoke to Adam:
"Tend my gairden wi care,
And aet o' the fruit
O' the trees that growe there.

"The fig-tree, the olive,
The grapes on the vine,
And a'thing that growes
In the gairden are thine.

"But *one* tree in the gairden
I keep to mysel:
The tree o' the knowledge
Of good and of ill.

"Its fruit is forbidden
Forever," said he.
"On the day that ye touch it
Ye surely shall dee."

And Adam was pleased
In the gairden to dwell,
But whiles he grew lonely
Bein aa by himsel.

So as Adam lay sleepin
Ae nicht on the grun
God made him a wife
Fae his ain flesh and bone.

When he waukened next mornin
And opened his eyes
He thocht that a star
Had come doon fae the skies:

For the loveliest creature
That ever he'd seen
Was knelt by his side
On the carpet o' green.

He had never imagined
Such pure loveliness:
"Bone of my bones,
And flesh of my flesh."

And so shall a man
Leave his father and mither,
And cleave to his wife
To mak one flesh thegither.

And thegither they'd walk
In the sun-dappled groves
By the cool crystal river
And speak o' their love.

Their innocent pleasures
To sit in the sun,
Jist bein thegither
When a'thing was young.

And the sounds o' the watters
Would lull them to rest
As saftly the sunset
Grew pale in the West.

But the serpent was sleekit,
Maist sleekit ava,
And he bided his time
Till her man went awa;

Syne he slithered up slyly
As Eve sat hersel,
And he whispered his words
In a voice that was fell:

PLATE *1*

Let there be Licht

PLATE *2*

Eve

"The tree o' the knowledge
Of good and of ill,
The tree that God wants
To keep aa to himsel:

"Its fruit's good and wholesome;
It can open your eyes
And mak ye like Gods,
All-powerful and wise.

"Did ye say that God telt ye,
If ye eat it ye die?
He's jist said that to stop ye;
He kens it's a lie."

"But wait! tell me mair.
Is there nae risk ava?"
But the silver-tongued serpent
Had slithered awa.

When they tasted the fruit
O' the forbidden tree
They felt guilty and sad:
They were nae langer free,

And their innocent pleasures
Could be never the same.
They sewed fig-leaves thegither
To cover their shame.

In the cool o' the evenin
Through the musk-scented vales
In the Gairden o' Eden
God came walkin himsel.

But of Adam and Eve
Not a trace could be seen.
God cried oot his name:
"Adam, whar hae ye gaen?"

"O Lord, when we heard ye
We hid in the trees,
For ye see . . . we're baith naked."
Adam fell to his knees.

And the Lord God was grieved
For he kent whar they'd been:
Sin had entered the world.
"Adam, what hae ye deen?"

"Lord, I ate fae the tree
That ye keep to yoursel.
My wife made me dee it."
Eve was tremblin and pale.

"Eve, what hae ye deen?
The fruit o' the tree?"
"Lord, the serpent deceived me,
And I took it," said she.

God spoke to the serpent:
"*Forever be cursed!*
You will crawl on your belly
And aet o' the dust.

"You will crawl on your belly
Till the day that ye're deid;
And the seed o' the woman
Will trample your heid."

And God spoke to the woman:
"In sorrow and pain
Will ye bring forth your children."
Eve wept in her shame.

And to Adam he said:
"You have disobeyed me,
And aeten the fruit
O' the forbidden tree.

"In sorrow and pain
Will ye chauve aa your days,
And aet fae the grun
In the sweat o' your face.

"In sorrow and pain
Till ye lie in the grun,
For fae dust were ye ta'en
And to dust will return."

And God banished them baith
Fae the gairden forever,
Fae the sun-dappled groves
And the cool crystal river;

To wander the earth
And to work on the grun,
And mind on the days
When a'thing was young.

Noah's Ark

The race o' men had multiplied
And spread owre aa the land;
But men regarded not the Lord,
Nor followed his commands.

Their wyes were full o' wickedness,
Their herts were full o' hate;
It grieved God sair to see his world
In sic a sorry state.

He regretted his Creation
And the day he'd gien man breath.
"I'll destroy the race o' men," he said.
"I will wipe them fae the earth.

"And this doom will fa' on a'thing
For the evil man has done:
Aa birds and beasts and creepin things
That live upon the grun."

One man there was ca'd Noah,
An upright man and wise,
A righteous man and blameless,
That found favour in God's eyes.

God said to Noah: "Build an ark,
That ye micht escape my wrath;
For a muckle flood will come
To destroy aa life on earth.

"It's timmers mak o' cypress wood.
Build it strong and build it fast,
Wi lower, mid and upper decks;
Nae need for spars or mast.

"And a bit abeen the gunnels
Pit a cover owre the decks;
Ye'd better mak it high
'Cause giraffes have got lang necks.

"Pitch it in and pitch it oot
To mak it watterticht;
Ye'll need a winda on the tap
To let ye hae some licht.

"Set a hatch into the gunnels
For loadin stores and gear;
Ye'll need plenty room for stores:
Tak enough to dee an 'ear.

"Ye winna need an anchor
For the landfalls will be few.
Your wife and your good-dothers
And your louns can be the crew.

"And o' every livin craitur
Tak a female and a male:
Aa birds and beasts and creepin things;
Ox, lion, moose and quail.

"Ye'll need plenty hay and fodder,
And every kind o' maet,
For aa the different craiturs
Maun hae something they can aet."

So Noah started buildin,
A lang and weary task;
But his louns came roon to help 'im,
And they got it deen at last.

The weemenfolk had gaithered maet
And fodder for them aa:
It took them near a fortnicht
Jist to get it stowed awa.

The folk aa came fae miles aroon
To lauch at Noah's ark.
They'd never seen the like afore;
It towered abeen the park.

They were nearly finished stowein
The final load o' hay,
When Ham shouted till his father:
"What's yon comin doon the brae?"

A hale jing-bang o' animals,
The like ye never saw,
Cam doon the brae towards the ark;
They were marchin twa by twa.

There was sheep and goats and cattle,
And horses, dogs and cats;
There was chimpanzees and camels,
Hedgehogs, buffaloes and bats.

There was elephants and tigers,
Giraffes and kangaroos;
There was snakes and bears and lizards,
And mice and pygmy shrews.

There was scorpions and beetles
O' every shape and size;
Centipedes and horny gollachs,
And moths and butterflies.

And every kind o' animal,
I canna name them aa,
Climmed up the ramp into the ark;
They were marchin twa by twa.

And abeen them flew the birds:
There was budgies, storks and doos;
And linties, larks and sparras,
Eagles, cras and cockatoos.

And aa the tribes o' feathered folk
Fae mountain, dale and park;
Aa fleein twa by twa they came
To roost in Noah's ark.

When aa the birds and animals
Were safe aboord the ark,
Noah and his faimly jined them;
The sky was growein dark.

The thunder rolled, the lichtnin flashed,
The rain cam doon in sheets;
The heavens' floodgates opened,
And the springs o' the great deep.

For forty days the rain cam doon;
It fell and never ceased
Till a'thing on the earth was drooned:
Aa men, aa birds, aa beasts.

The watters rose owre aa the earth,
Owre valley, plain and wood;
The vera highest mountains
Were sunk aneth the flood.

The hale o' God's Creation
Sunk till a wattery grave;
The ark alone in aa the world
Upon the empty waves.

At last the rain abated;
The storm clouds cleared awa;
A wind blew on the watters
And the flood began to fa'.

Ae day when Noah was on watch
The ark began to heel;
He felt the scrape o' solid grun
Hard underneath her keel.

He ran on deck. "Praise God!" he cried.
"I winner whar we're at?"
Noah's ark had come to rest
On the hills o' Ararat.

He sent oot a muckle raven;
It soared into the sky,
But jist kept fleein back and fore
Till aa the earth was dry.

Then Noah let a doo gang free
To look for land ana';
She circled twice aroon the ark
Afore she flew awa.

But still the endless watters streetched
Owre mountain, dale and park.
She found nae place to rest her fit
And flew back to the ark.

Next time he let the doo awa
She circled once and flew.
That nicht when she came back to him
She brocht a welcome clue:

An olive leaf was in her beak,
It was freshly-plucked and green;
Noah kent the worst was ower
And his work was nearly deen.

Next time she never circled once
But flew baith high and fast.
She never socht the ark again:
Noah kent the flood was past.

They disembarked the animals;
The birds soared in the blue;
God's rainbow shone abeen the clouds,
And aa the world was new.

Moses

The Pharaoh's daughter came to bathe
Doon by the banks o' Nile,
Along the willow-cloistered path,
A green and livin aisle.

And in the lily-dappled pool,
Screened fae the noonday heat,
She blessed the watter, clear and cool,
And dipped her slender feet.

She drowsed there in the emerald glow
That filtered through the trees,
When suddenly a bairnie's cry
Disturbed her reverie.

Among the flags and bulrushes
That lined the watter's edges
She saw a basket floatin,
Half-hidden in the sedges.

Gently rockin on the watter,
It lay jist oot o' reach.
She sent her maid to fetch it,
And bring it to the beach.

She opened up the basket;
The bairnie gave a cry.
"*It's a little Hebrew lounie*
That someone's left to die!"

Her woman's hert went oot to him.
"Peer craitur, what's adee?
Did they leave ye here yoursel then?
Will I tak ye hame wi me?"

At this a little quine ran up;
She'd been watchin fae the trees.
"I could get a Hebrew woman, ma'am,
To nurse him, if ye please?"

She'd been watchin since that mornin,
Since her mither went awa,
Watchin owre her little brither
To see what would befa.

Pharaoh had issued a decree:
That every little loun
Born till a Hebrew mither
Be ta'en awa and drooned.

Ae woman kept her little loun
For three months in the hoose,
Hidden fae the Pharaoh's sodjers.
But she kent it was nae use:

Ae day they'd come and find him,
And she kent what it would be.
So she bocht a bulrush basket;
There was naething else to dee.

She covered it wi mud and pitch
To mak it watterticht;
Then she went doon to the river
Jist as it was gettin licht.

It broke her hert to leave her bairn
In a basket in the rushes.
But her lassie bade to watch;
She was hidin in the bushes.

The princess turned and smiled
At the little Hebrew maid.
"That's exactly what I need;
Gang and fetch a nurse," she said.

So the lassie brocht her mither
To come and nurse the bairn.
The princess rose to meet them;
He was cradled in her airms.

"My good woman," said the princess,
"Here's a little Hebrew child
That I want ye to bring up for me;
I found him in the Nile.

"Tak and love him like your ain,
And I'll pay ye well," said she.
"Then when he's a bittie auler
Ye must bring him back to me."

His mither took him hame again
Till he grew up tall and strong.
Pharaoh's daughter ca'd him Moses,
And she took him for her son.

Crossing the Red Sea

The Israelites had made their camp
On the shores o' the Red Sea,
Whar the Hand o' God had led them
Aifter Pharaoh set them free.

By day a muckle cloud o' smoke
Went afore them in the sky,
And by nicht a fiery pillar
To lead them on their wye.

But now the cloud stood still
Afore them in the East,
They were gled to rest a while:
Man, bairn, and weary beast.

For their journey had been sair:
Fleein fae the Pharaoh's rage,
By rocky paths and steeny wyes,
Along the desert's edge.

He'd been gled to see the back o' them:
What, wi rivers turned to bleed;
Wi puddocks, flees and locusts;
Then his firstborn son had deed.

But Pharaoh's hert was hardened
Now the Israelites had gaen;
He had naebody to dig ditches,
Build his roads, or quarry stane.

So he set aff wi his army:
Chariots, foot, and mounted men,
To chase the fleein Israelites
And bring them back again.

Fae their camp doon by the watter
They saw the chariots come,
Foremost rank o' Pharaoh's army,
Weapons glintin in the sun.

The folk aa turned on Moses.
"*Now* what ye gaun to dee?
Wi sea afore and hills ahin,
There's naewye left to flee.

"Was there nae graves left in Egypt
That ye brocht us here to dee?
We were better aff as slaves;
Ye should've let us be."

"Fear not!" said Moses. "Trust the Lord;
He rules the fates o' men.
The army that ye see this day,
Ye will never see again."

God spoke to Moses: "Lift your staff
And haud it owre the sea
That the watters may roll back,
And my people shall gang free."

At this, God's sign in front o' them,
The cloudy pillar rose;
And came back doon to earth again
Atween them and their foes.

It loured owre the Pharaoh's camp
Wi blackest shades o' nicht:
But on the Hebrew camp it shone,
A clear, effulgent licht.

Syne Moses lifted up his staff
And streetchit oot his hand;
A strong wind blew the watters back
And the sea bed was dry land.

The Hebrews made the crossin
Throwe the eerie ocean-pass;
The watters surged abeen their heids,
Sheer cliffs o' sapphire glass.

Pharaoh's army tried to follow:
Chariots, troops, and cavalry;
But they foonert in the weet sand
In the middle o' the sea.

The chariot-wheels sank deeper;
Horses whinnied, sodjers cried;
But they couldna trace their steps again,
Nor win the ither side.

The stragglers o' the Israelites
Had reached the further shore;
Moses lifted up his staff;
There came an awesome roar

As the muckle cliffs o' watter
Toppled owre and filled the void,
Crushin a'thing underneath them:
Pharaoh's army was destroyed.

Thus did God preserve his people
By the shores o' the Red Sea,
When he led them oot o' Egypt
Aifter Pharaoh set them free.

Samson and Delilah

The prisoner was manacled
To the wheel that grinds the grain,
And roon and roon his weary course
He plodded in his chains.

Fae brak o' sky he'd plod his wye
Till evenin shadows came;
But day and nicht, and dark and bricht
To him were aa the same.

The Philistines would come to mock
The blin man in his chains:
"Is this the mighty *Samson*?
Reduced to grindin grain?

"*Samson*, the mighty man o' war,
In manacles and chains?
Samson, the lion-killer?"
They lauched to see his pain.

At last the hateful day would end,
And the hateful nicht begin.
He'd mind aboot the happy times
Afore they'd made him blin:

Delilah o' the raven locks;
Delilah's lovely face;
Delilah o' the slender form;
He'd loved her lichtsome grace.

He'd lie there in his prison cell
And mind on times lang gaen;
The sunshine o' the past jist made
The present blacker seem.

PLATE *3*

Noah

PLATE *4*

Moses

He minded when he saw her first,
The stars were in his eyes;
He'd loved her fae that vera day,
His jewel beyond price.

When she became his lover,
How happy had he been.
He minded on her gentle wyes;
Delilah was his queen.

And how she liked to tease him;
It seemed a silly game:
Aye askin whar he got his strength,
And how he could be tamed.

He'd played the game to humour her.
"If ye tie me up wi string,
I'm as helpless as a kittlin,
As weak as onything."

She waited till he fell asleep,
Syne tied him up wi string;
But Samson woke and snapped it
As quick as onything.

He lauched to see her sulky face.
"*You lied to me*," said she.
"Ye would tell me aa your secrets
If ye really cared for me."

"A'richt," said he, still lauchin.
"This time I'll tell ye true:
The only wye to bind me
Is to use a rope that's new."

Next nicht, as he lay sleepin,
She tied him ticht indeed;
But Samson woke and broke the rope
As easy as 'twere threid.

"Ye really dinna love me,
Or ye wouldna tell me lies.
Ye only mak a feel o' me."
The tears were in her eyes.

Day aifter day she nagged at him;
It got him doon at length.
"A'richt," said he, "I'll tell ye
The secret o' my strength.

"I was brocht up a Nazarite
Since the day that I was born:
My strength lies in my seven locks
That never hae been shorn.

"If I should tak a razor
And shave my heid aa bare,
I should be weak as ither men;
My strength lies in my hair."

Ae nicht she cradled him to sleep
Wi his heid upon her knee,
For the wine had made him drowsy.
"Sweet dreams, my love," said she.

He wandered throwe an empty land
Whar aa the trees were bare;
Nae sang o' bird, nae breath o' wind
Disturbed the silence there.

He was lookin for Delilah.
He shouted oot her name.
A mockin echo fae the hills,
The only answer came.

Lang time he wandered in his dream
Throwe empty vale and wood.
He came across a hidden stream,
And there Delilah stood:

Mair radiant and mair lovely
Than he'd ever seen afore.
She gently beckoned him to cross
Owre to the further shore.

"Come, Samson. Come to me, my love."
He stepped into the stream;
The watters closed abeen his heid;
He waukened fae his dream.

His airms were bound, his legs were tied;
He struggled to get free.
Delilah stood in front o' him.
"Too late, my love," said she.

A caul chill gripped his hert wi fear
When he saw what she had done:
His seven locks lay on the fleer;
His mighty strength was gone.

He minded on her staunin there,
The last thing that he'd seen:
He screamed and fainted wi the pain
As they gouged oot his een.

They took him doon to Gaza
In manacles and chains;
A beast o' burden, blin and weak,
Reduced to grindin grain.

Lang, weary miles o' endless nicht
He chauved to grind the grain;
But the hair upon his shaven heid
Began to growe again.

The leaders o' the Philistines
Had gaithered in the hall
To praise their great god, Dagon,
In a mighty festival;

To praise him for their triumph
And the doonfa o' their foe.
They dragged Samson fae his prison
And pit him oot on show.

In the hall, atween the pillars,
He stood there in his chains.
The folk aa jeered and taunted him,
And ca'd him filthy names.

"Ye orra Jewish scum!" they cried.
"Aye, whar's your strength at noo?
Samson the *lion-killer!*
He couldna kill a coo!"

Samson askit at the lounie
Wha had led him fae the jile:
"Pit my hauns upon the pillars;
I need to rest a while."

He bowed his heid and prayed to God:
"O Lord, remember me.
Please gie me back my strength again,
Jist *once* afore I dee;

"That I may be revenged on them
That took awa my een.
My auld strength back this one last time,
O Lord, and then I'm deen."

He grasped the pillars in his hauns,
Samson the Nazarite.
"*Let me die wi the Philistines!*"
He pushed wi aa his might.

The sinews stood oot on his neck;
The sweat ran doon his back;
The Philistines aa lauched and jeered;
There came a mighty *crack* . . .

The pillars broke; the temple fell
On the jeerin crowd aneth.
The Nazarite had been revenged:
Victorious in his death.

David and Goliath

Young David was a shepherd,
Unkent to power or fame,
The youngest son o' Jesse
In the toun o' Bethlehem.

Whar the mountain grass was greenest
In the howes among the rocks,
By the quaet upland watters
He would lead his father's flocks.

And at nicht he'd play his harp
And sing a shepherd's tune,
When the mountains towered abeen him,
Silvered in the risin moon.

His aulder brithers went to fecht
Wi the men o' Israel
In the war against the Philistines,
In the army o' King Saul.

Ae day his father said to him,
"It's a whilie since we heard
Fae your brithers in the army;
Gang and bring me back some word.

"There's loafs and cheese and roastit grain
To tak to them as well.
Keep ye weel back fae the fechtin,
Now mind; and watch yoursel."

Next mornin, bright and early,
David set aff on his wye;
He was weel along the road
Or the sun rose in the sky.

When he reached the Jewish camp
The men were marchin forth
To tak up their positions
On the high grun to the North.

He gaed pushin throwe the sodjers
Till he reached the forward lines,
Whar the army o' King Saul
Faced the ranks o' Philistines

Wi a valley in atween them.
War cries rent the mornin air
As the hosts prepared for battle,
And he found his brithers there.

"*David!* What ye deein here?"
His auldest brither cried.
"This is nae place for a lounie!"
Suddenly the shoutin died.

The hosts o' Israel fell dumb;
A murmur swept their lines
As a giant steppit forward
Fae the ranks o' Philistines.

The giant was Goliath,
A Philistine fae Gath;
He towered nine feet abeen the grun,
And fearsome was his wrath.

A muckle sword hung by his side,
A spear was in his haun;
Its shaft was like a weaver's rod,
It glinted in the sun.

His voice rolled oot like thunder
As he strode along the brae:
"Come, aa you men o' Israel;
Wha will fecht wi me this day?

"Come, choose ye oot a champion
To fecht me, man to man;
And if your man should kill me,
Oor fate is in your hauns:

"The Philistines will serve ye.
But if *I* win the fray,
Then *we* shall be your maisters.
Wha will fecht wi me this day?"

The Israelites were terrified;
Their finest sodjers quailed.
Wha could stand against this giant
In his coat o' shinin mail?

"I will fecht you," shouted David,
"For the Lord is on my side."
His brithers were astonished.
"*Haud your wisht!*" the auldest cried.

"You're jist here to steer up trouble;
G'wa back to your sheep again.
Run awa hame to your mither;
Leave the fechtin to the men."

But the shepherd loun persisted;
Seen he stood afore the king.
"Please sir, let me fecht the giant;
I will fecht him wi my sling,

And the Lord will gie me victory."
Saul looked him up and doon.
"I canna let ye fecht *him*:
Ye're jist a wee bit loun.

"This Philistine's a fechtin man,
And has been fae his youth;
The foremost o' their champions,
And *nine fit high*, forsooth!"

"But sir, I guard my father's flocks,
On the shieling up the brae;
I have killed baith bear and lion
When the wild beast cam to prey.

"This muckle heathen Philistine
Will fa' like ane o' them;
The Lord that saved me fae the beasts
Will deliver me fae him."

"A'richt," said Saul. "God gang wi ye
Against the Philistine.
We'd better get some mail for ye;
Here, try this suit o' mine."

Syne David tried the armour on,
And clanked aroon a while.
"I canna fecht like this", he said:
"The weicht will cramp my style.

"I must be free to move, ye see;
My safety lies in speed.
My shepherd's staff, and five smooth stanes,
And sling are aa 't I need."

He took the armour aff again,
Perspirin wi its weight;
Syne chose five stanes fae oot the burn
And went to meet his fate.

The men aroon fell back in awe
As he marched oot throwe their lines:
A fresh-faced, unfledged shepherd loun
Against the Philistine.

Goliath roared wi lauchter:
"Are *you* their chosen man?
The champion o' Israel;
The best in aa the land?

"Ye're jist a shepherd lounie!
Get awa back to your herds;
Or, by the great god, Dagon,
I'll feed ye to the birds!"

But David faced the Philistine.
"You come wi spear and sword
Against the hosts o' Israel,
The armies o' the Lord:

"I come against ye in *his* name,
That name that ye defied.
This day I'll fecht and kill ye,
For the Lord is on my side."

The giant's rage was terrible:
He shook his muckle spear;
He'd gar this little upstart pey,
And gar him pey full dear.

"Div ye think that I'm a *dog*,
To chase wi sticks and stanes?
Come ower here, ye little vratch,
And I'll pulverize your banes!"

Goliath moved in for the kill
As David slung his steen;
It struck the giant on the heid,
Full in atween the een.

The spear fell eeseless at his feet;
He toppled to the grun.
The giant Philistine was beat;
The shepherd loun had won.

He ran to whar his vanquished foe
Lay in a pool o' bleed;
He drew the giant's muckle sword
And chappit aff his heid.

The hosts o' Israel aa cheered
As he raised the drippin heid;
The Philistines aa fled the field,
For their champion was deid.

David and Bathsheba

The king had sent his men to war
Against the Ammonites,
Wi his trusted general, Joab,
To lead them in the fight.

Joab's army was victorious.
When the heathen army fell
He besieged the toun o' Rabbah
Wi the men o' Israel.

The king was on his palace roof;
The sun was sinkin doon;
The West was streaked wi reed and gold
As nicht fell on the toun.

The scent o' musk and jasmine
Hung in the evenin air.
He lookit owre the gairdens
And he saw her staunin there,

By a pool among the willows,
As she dried her silken hair.
He was smitten wi her beauty
And could only stand and stare.

Such elegance of slender form,
Such loveliness of face;
An angel bathin in a pool;
Such eloquence of grace.

Enchanted wi her beauty,
Lang aifter she had gaen
He stood and stared into the nicht
Wi blank, unseein een.

Like ane wha wanders in a dream
The king spoke till himsel:
"Such loveliness I've never seen.
I want her for mysel."

His servant telt King David:
"Bathsheba is her name.
Her husband is Uriah;
She's waitin for him hame.

"He's at the war wi Joab
And the ither Israelites,
In the army o' the king
Against the Ammonites."

"Gang fetch this woman for me,
And bring her to my bed.
I value your discretion;
Tell naebody else," he said.

Bathsheba stood wi dooncast een,
Ashamed afore the king.
"O lord, please dinna mak me;
This is an evil thing."

But kings, like knaves, will hae their wye
When fleshly passions move.
Wi honeyed words he soothed her qualms:
They spent the nicht in love.

Bathsheba sent the king this word:
"Aa the folk will ken my shame,
For now I gang wi bairn, my lord,
And my husband nae at hame."

The king sent for Uriah
To come and bring him word
Aboot the siege o' Rabbah,
And how his sodjers fared.

He telt the king aboot the war
And a'thing that had passed.
The king was pleased and thanked him:
"Now tak your ease at last.

"Well done my faithfu' servant.
Now rest ye fae the fecht;
Gang hame and sleep ye weel", he said,
"In your ain bed this nicht."

Uriah never socht his wife
Though the nicht was gettin late,
But wrapped him in a blanket
Doon by the palace gate.

Next mornin David sent for him
When he heard whar he had lain.
"Why slept ye by the palace gate,
And never socht your hame?"

"My lord, I will dee nae such thing:
When aa my maister's men
Are camped oot in the open fields,
How could I seek my hame?

"When aa the hosts o' Israel
Are fechtin in the strife,
How could I aet and drink at hame,
And lie there wi my wife?"

"*My good and faithfu' servant!*
Bide here for one mair day.
The nicht ye'll aet and drink wi me;
And dinna say me nay."

That nicht King David made him drunk
And bad him seek his hame,
But still Uriah made his bed
By the palace gate again.

A loyal man and honest;
A noble man was he.
King David cursed his goodness;
What was he gaun to dee?

But honesty's a peer defence
For treachery and hate.
Uriah's days were numbered;
His honour sealed his fate.

When he left the toun next mornin
He bore a deadly note
Fae David to his general.
And this is what he wrote:

"Set Uriah in the vanguard
In the fiercest o' the fight,
Then cry back your ither sodjers
And leave him till his plight,

"That he may be struck doon and dee.
I trust you in this thing;
And mind, mak nae mistakes, Joab.
I am your lord, the king."

And so Joab arranged it,
As his maister had decreed.
He sent this word to David:
"My lord, your servant's deid.

"A brave man and a true was he;
He focht well for your cause.
But they struck him fae the battlements:
He was too close to the wa's."

When Bathsheba heard the news
She grieved her husband sair;
Her bonny een were swelled wi tears
For the man she'd see nae mair.

David brocht her to the palace
When her mournin-time was done.
Syne he took her for his wife,
And she bore to him a son.

Nathan the prophet. Tall and stern
He stood afore the throne;
His locks were white, his beard was lang,
His eyes as hard as stone.

"There were twa men, O king," said he,
"Lived in a certain toun;
The ane was rich, the ither peer."
King David lookit doon.

"The rich had mony flocks and herds:
The peer man, ae yowe lamb.
He loved it like a vera bairn,
And fed it fae his haun.

PLATE *5*

David and Goliath

PLATE *6*

David and Bathsheba

"A traiveller came to the rich man
And socht for maet and rest;
He stole the peer man's ae yowe lamb
And killed it for his guest."

"*What man is this?*" roared oot the king.
"That man shall surely dee!
For he has deen an evil thing.
Come, tell me, *wha is he?*"

"*You are that man!*" the seer replied,
"That did this evil thing,
Abhorrent in the sicht o' God.
You are that man, O king!

"Ye hae despised the livin God
And ta'en a just man's life:
Ye slew Uriah wi the sword,
And stole your servant's wife.

"And by the sword your grief will come,
Baith treachery and strife:
For ane fae your ain hoose, O king,
Will rise and tak your wifes.

"You did this thing in secret,
In the darkness o' the nicht:
But he that comes to tak your wifes
Will dee't in broad daylicht."

The king bowed low in penitence.
"I hae sinned, O Lord," said he.
"The Lord has ta'en awa your sin;
But Bathsheba's son will dee."

The prophet spoke and left the king.
The king would pray and fast;
But a'thing that was prophesied
That day would come to pass.

Solomon's Judgement

The royal court was crowded
Wi folk on every side.
Twa weemen stood afore the throne
To hear their cases tried.

The first ane stood wi dooncast een,
Pale face and tremblin lip:
The second glowered wi brazen looks,
Her hauns upon her hips.

The young king looked them up and doon
Syne lookit at his feet:
Twa bairnies lay in knitted shawls;
Ae bairn began to greet.

The ither bairnie never moved;
Its limbs were stiff and caul:
The first ane roared and kicked its feet
And warsled in its shawl.

Ae woman moved to pick it up;
A guard stood in atween.
The ither woman glowered at her
Wi hard, unflinchin een.

"Ye see, my lord," spoke up the wife,
"The justice o' my case.
She even tries to tak my bairn
Afore your vera face!

"She's jist a sleekit, orra vratch,
As aa the toun weel kens.
She only wants to steal my bairn
'Cause her ain was overlain."

"Not so, my lord," spoke up the first.
"*That* woman's bairnie's dead;
She stole mine as I lay asleep.
I speak the truth," she said.

The young king sat and stroked his beard;
He pondered lang and sair.
He lookit at the livin bairn;
He lookit at the pair.

"Ane says, *My bairnie's livin,*
And hers the ane that died;
The ither says, *Not so, my lord*:
A hard case to decide."

At length he stood and faced the court.
"*Bring me a sword!*" he cried.
"Since baith are wantin't, baith shall hae't:
A half to either side!"

The captain o' the guard came in,
The sword drawn fae his sheath;
A murmur swept the crowded court;
They stared in disbelief.

A dreadful silence filled the court;
The sword was lifted high.
"Lord, spare my bairn! Gie it to *her!*
I canna watch him die."

At once the king held up his haun.
"*Stop!* There's a mither's word.
The livin bairnie's hers," he said.
The captain sheathed his sword.

King Solomon picked up the bairn
And gave it till its mither.
She bowed her heid and thanked him:
"God bless your hoose forever."

The crowded court was silent,
For the folk were overawed
By the wisdom o' the king,
And they kent it came fae God.

Naaman

Now Naaman was a general,
A valiant man o' might,
Wha led the Syrian army
Against the Israelites.

He was honoured by the king
And his men held him in awe;
But Naaman was a leper:
His single, tragic flaw.

His wife had a maidservant,
A little Hebrew quine;
She'd been captured by the Syrians
In a raid on Palestine.

Ae day she came to Naaman's wife.
"I ken a man", said she,
"Wha could cure my master's illness
And heal his leprosy:

"A prophet in Samaria,
Elisha is his name.
My lord should gang and see him;
He bides aside my hame."

When the king was telt the good news
O' the little Hebrew maid
He was filled wi hope for Naaman.
"Ye must gang at once," he said.

"Tak ye gifts o' gold and silver
And gang to Israel.
Ye'll need a letter for the king;
I'll write to him mysel."

The king o' Israel looked up
And an angry man was he.
"Daes your maister think that I'm a *God*,
That he sends ye doon to me?

"He jist wants to pick a fecht!
What am *I* supposed to dee?"
Naaman lookit at the grun.
Was he doomed to leprosy?

"*A letter fae Elisha, Sire.*"
The herald bowed his head
And handed owre the parchment.
And this is what it said:

"Send me the Syrian general
And dinna fash yoursel;
For he shall ken a prophet lives
In the land o' Israel."

Naaman waited by his chariot
Ootside the prophet's hame.
At last the door was opened
And oot a servant came.

"Gang ye doon to Jordan's watters
Seven times and wash yoursel;
Then your leprosy will leave ye
And your flesh shall be made hale."

But Naaman lost the heid at this.
"I've traivelled aa this wye;
And now ye say to *wash mysel!*
Whar's your maister onywye?

"He could surely come and see me;
That's the least that he could dee.
I thocht he'd come and wave his hauns
And cure my leprosy.

"If I'd wanted to gang sweemin,
I would've stayed at hame.
The Jordan's jist a muddy burn;
We've got better o' wir ain."

He stormed aboord his chariot
And gaithered up the reins;
But his servant checked his haun.
"My lord, please think again.

"Had he telt ye something difficult,
Would ye nae hae tried to dee't?
Ye should gang and wash in Jordan;
The worst ye'll get is weet."

So Naaman went and dipped himsel
Seven times in Jordan's stream;
And his skin was like a bairn's,
For his leprosy was gaen.

He went back to Elisha.
"Please accept these gifts fae me.
Your power has healed your servant's flesh
And cured his leprosy."

"I canna tak your gifts, my loun:
The Lord has healed, not I."
The prophet smiled and took his haun.
"Praise God, and gang your wye."

And Naaman fell doon on his knees.
"The God o' Israel
Shall be my God for evermair;
I'll worship him mysel."

The Fiery Furnace

The statue glinted in the sun,
Full fifteen fathoms high;
Abeen the plains o' Babylon
It towered into the sky.

Its muckle form was clad in gold
Wi pagan runes engraved;
Its evil features, hard and cold,
Struck terror in the brave.

And aa the folk were gathered there
By order o' the king:
Officials, rulers, sodjers, slaves,
To dedicate the thing.

The herald's voice rang loud and clear:
"This is the king's decree:
Aa folk will bow and worship here
On pain o' death," said he.

"When music sounds fae horn and flute,
Fae trumpet, harp and lyre,
Fa' doon afore the golden god,
Or perish in the fire!"

A deathly hush fell on the crowd
On the plains o' Babylon.
The sudden music blared oot loud;
The folk fell doon as one.

They fell afore the golden god;
As far as eye could see
Their prostrate forms sprawled owre the plain
Whar aa had fa'n, but three.

Tall, prood and brave they stood there,
Alone against the sky.
They'd *never* bow to heathen gods:
A Jew would seener die!

But jealous een were watchin
And brocht the king the news.
"Aa folk hae fa'n and worshipped, Sire;
But still three men refuse.

"Three o' your highest counsellors,
Ye promoted them yoursel:
Shadrach, Meshach, Abednego,
Fae the land o' Israel."

The three stood there afore the king.
"Well? Is it true?" said he.
"Div ye still refuse to worship?
Ye ken the penalty:

"A fiery furnace is the fate
O' them that winna bow.
Shadrach, Meshach, Abednego,
Tell me your answer *now!*"

The Hebrews didna hesitate
To mak him this reply:
"We'll *never* bow to heathen gods,
O king: we'd seener die!

"The one true God we worship,
The God o' Israel,
Wha hauds aa kingdoms in his haun,
Can save us, if he will.

"But if he will or winna,
Let us mak oor meanin clear:
We'll never serve your gods, O king;
Nae in a thoosan year!"

Nebuchadnezzar paled wi rage;
He leapt up wi a roar:
"*Mak the fiery furnace hetter
Than it's ever been afore!*

"Seize them and cast them in the fire!
Ungrateful Jewish scum!
What god can save ye now", he cried,
"Fae the fires o' Babylon?"

They took and bound them, hauns and feet,
And threw them in the door;
The guards were struck doon deid wi heat
Sae fierce the furnace roared.

The king watched in amazement.
"But surely there was *three*;
We tied them up and flung them in.
There's four inside!" cried he.

"In the middle o' the furnace
They walk unscathed and free;
The fourth is like the Son o' God,
Radiant in majesty."

The king ran to the furnace door.
"Come oot! come oot!" cried he.
"Shadrach, Meshach, Abednego,
Come ower here to me."

The three stepped through the furnace door
And stood afore the king;
They never even smelt o' reek,
And nae a hair was singed.

"Ye servants o' the Maist High God,
I bless his holy name,
Wha sent his angel doon this day
And saved ye fae the flames.

"Ye walkit throwe the flames o' death
Afore ye'd serve anither:
Now ye shall serve your God in peace,
And worship him forever."

The Writing on the Wall

The king was in his banquet hall
Drinkin the bleed-reed wine
Wi a thoosan o' his nobles,
His wifes and concubines.

They cried for maet, they cried for drink,
They shouted in their glee;
The reed wine flowed, the king's cheek glowed,
And a drunken man was he.

"Bring me the golden drinkin cups
Fae the temple o' the Jews.
I hae a mind to drink fae them;
We'll pit them to good use."

The sacred cups his father stole
These mony years lang syne:
The vessels fae the house o' God
To haud the pagan wine.

The cups were brocht; the wine was poored;
Up stood the king sae bold.
"We'll drink a toast, my noble guests:
To the gods, the gods o' gold."

The folk aa cheered; they drank the toast.
"Here's to the gods o' gold,
And silver, brass and iron,
Wir fathers' gods of old."

They praised the gods o' wood and stane
And drank to them ana',
When suddenly the king fell pale
And pinted at the wa'.

A sudden hush fell on the crowd;
A caul fear gripped them aa:
The fingers o' a ghostly haun
Were writin on the wa'.

The fingers wrote and vanished;
But the writin stood oot clear.
"*What trick is this?*" roared oot the king.
His body shook wi fear.

"Send for my best astrologers;
Send for my wise men aa
To read this ghastly sign for me
That's written on the wa'.

"Whaever reads this sign for me
And maks its meanin plain
I will clothe in robes o' scarlet,
He will weer a golden chain.

"His reward will be great honour,
And riches fae my hand;
He will govern in my kingdom,
The third in aa the land."

The wise men and astrologers
Stood and puzzled owre the thing,
But they couldna read the writin
Nor explain it to the king.

The king's cheek paled, his courage failed,
And a sober man was he.
"O whar will I get a soothsayer
To read this sign for me?"

"So pale, my lord," spoke up the queen,
"For such a little thing?
Be not dismayed: *I ken a man.*
Lift up your hert, O king.

"When your father ruled the kingdom
He was famed throughout the land
For his excellence o' wisdom,
Greater far than *ony* man.

"Your father, aye, your father,
Made him chief o' the wise men,
For readin dreams and riddles
And things beyond oor ken.

"They say the spirit o' the gods
Rests in this man, my lord.
Send for Daniel; he will tell ye
The meanin o' the words."

Then Daniel stood afore the throne.
"Are you Daniel the Jew,
That my father brocht fae Judah?
I have heard great things of you:

"That great light and understandin
And intelligence are thine;
Of your excellence of wisdom
And your power to read strange signs.

"My wise men canna help me;
My astrologers are dumb.
Wha can read this ghastly writin?
Tell me, Daniel, is there *none?*

"If ye read this writin for me
And mak its meanin plain,
I will gie ye robes o' scarlet,
Ye will weer a golden chain.

"Your reward will be great honour,
And riches fae my hand;
You will govern in my kingdom,
The third in aa the land."

"I want nae scarlet robes, O king;
Ye can keep your golden chain;
Yet I will read this writin
And mak its meanin plain.

"The Lord God reigns supreme,
And appointeth whom he will
To rule the kingdoms o' the earth;
His law endureth still.

"But you, O king Belshazzar,
In the folly o' your pride,
Have set at naught the Lord o' heaven
And have cast his laws aside.

"You defiled his sacred vessels,
And you praised your heathen gods,
Which neither see, nor hear, nor ken:
Paltry things o' stane and wood.

"But *one* God ye havena honoured:
The *true God* wha rules the earth,
Wha has aa men in his keepin,
In his haun your vera breath.

"And God's haun it was ye saw there,
And the words it wrote, O king:
Mene, mene, tekel, parsin.
I will make their meanin plain.

"*Mene*: Your kingdom now is at an end;
God has coonted oot its days.
Tekel: You have failed the final test
In the balance that God weighs.

"*Peres*: Your kingdom is divided,
As the writin has foretold,
To the Persians and the Medes,
Your enemies of old."

Daniel got his scarlet robe,
And he wore a golden chain;
But that nicht the Medes attacked,
And King Belshazzar was slain.

Jonah

A message came to Jonah,
A message fae the Lord:
"Arise and gang to Nineveh
And preach the folk my word,

"For their sin has come afore me
And the evil o' their days.
I'll destroy their mighty city
If they dinna mend their ways."

Thocht Jonah, 'I'm nae prophet.
Has he naebody else to send?
Why should I gang and preach God's word
To folk I dinna ken?

'I'll mak my wye to Joppa,
And I'll run awa to sea.
I'm nae gaun to preach to heathens!
I've got better things to dee.'

So he made his wye to Joppa,
And lyin at the quay
Was a ship bound down for Tarshish,
Far across the Middle Sea.

They hadna gaen a league fae shore,
A league but barely twa,
When the sky began to lour
And the wind began to blaw.

They hadna gaen a league fae shore,
A league but barely three,
When they thocht their wifes and bairns
They never mair would see.

For the wind howled like a banshee
In the fierceness o' the gale,
As the demons o' the tempest
Clawed the spars and tore the sail.

And the seas cam doon like wild beasts,
Black wolves howlin fae the North,
Hungry for the lives o' sailors,
Sweepin a'thing in their path.

The sailors started prayin
As they focht to save the ship.
"*Ditch the cargo!*" roared the captain.
"*Man the oars! Aa hands on deck!*"

But the mair they focht and struggled
The wilder grew the sea.
Jonah went up to the captain.
"This is aa because o' me.

"If ye dinna dee my biddin
Ye'll nae see dry land again.
Tak and throw me owre the side,
Or your prayers are aa in vain."

The captain looked at Jonah.
"Forty years I've gaen to sea,
And I've never lost a man yet.
Pull on the oars!" roared he.

But the tempest's force redoubled.
"*So be it!*" the captain cried.
"Lord, hae mercy on his soul.
Tak and throw him owre the side!"

At once the wind fell still again
And glassy calm the seas.
The sailors fell and thanked the Lord
Upon their bended knees.

But a muckle whaal appeared
And swallowed Jonah hale,
Syne dived doon to the ocean depths
Wi a flourish o' its tail.

Deep, deep it dived to the abyss
Whar never licht was seen,
And fearsome monsters prowl the nicht
Wi huge and luminous een.

Three days and nichts was Jonah
In the silent, livin tomb,
Till his prayer arose to heaven
Fae the empty, hopeless gloom:

"Oot fae the vera depths o' hell,
O Lord, I cry to thee.
Thou hast cast me in the boundless deep,
To the caverns o' the sea.

"The dark tide swirled aboot me,
Cauld as Death and black as Nicht;
To the bottoms o' the mountains
Was I banished fae thy sicht.

"To the bottoms o' the mountains
And the earth that barred me in,
Yet towards thy holy temple
Will I turn and look again.

PLATE 7

Jonah

PLATE *8*

They shall soar with wings as eagles

"When my life was ebbin fae me
Then my prayer arose to thee:
I will sacrifice with gladness,
And that I vowed I'll dee."

Jonah felt the surf aboot his legs;
He heard the breakers roar.
Dazzled by the splendid licht,
He struggled to the shore.

Again God spoke to Jonah:
"Gang to Nineveh," said he,
"And tell the folk my judgement,
And issue my decree:

"That my doom will fa' on Nineveh,
As lichtnin fae the skies.
I am the Lord Almighty,
All-powerful and Wise."

So Jonah went to Nineveh
And preached throughout the toun:
"In anither forty days
God's judgement will come doon."

They listened to his message
And repented o' their sin,
And turned them fae their evil wyes,
Fae the lowest to the king.

Wi contrite herts they socht the Lord;
Their prayers arose to heaven.
And God was pleased and spared the toun
Fae the judgement he had given.

But Jonah prayed again to God
For he wasna pleased ava.
"I *kent* that this would happen;
That's why I ran awa.

"Now I've been made to look a feel
Because ye let them be.
I beg thee, Lord, to tak my life;
It's best that I should dee."

As he sat there in the desert,
The sun beat on his heid.
He mourned aloud his weary fate:
"O I wish that I was deid."

A vine sprang up to shelter him;
He blessed the bonny tree,
And sat him doon aneth its shade
To see what God would dee.

Next mornin when the sun came up
It shrivelled up and died;
And Jonah grieved to see its fate.
"*My bonny tree!*" he cried.

God spoke to Jonah, gently now:
"You're sorry for a tree,
Which ye neither grew nor wattered.
Consider well", said he:

"There are six score thoosan souls
In the toun that ye can see;
If aa these folk should be destroyed,
How sorry I should be."

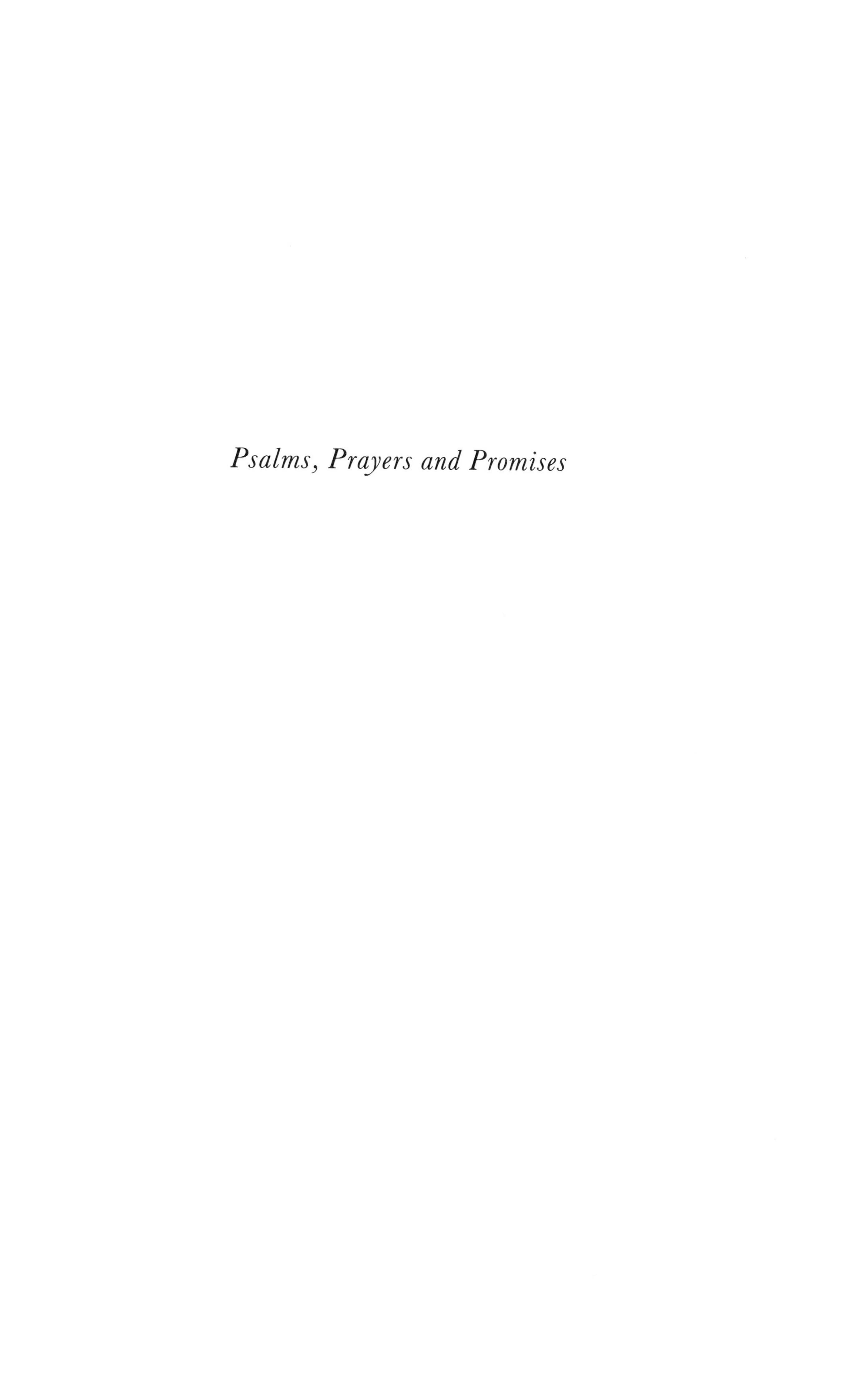

Psalms, Prayers and Promises

What is man?

O Lord our God, how excellent
Your name in aa the earth!
Abeen the heavens in splendour
Your majesty shines forth.

I contemplate the vault o' heaven,
Created by your haun,
The moon and stars that ye ordained,
And wonder, *What is man?*

What is he that ye mind on him?
And aa the sons o' men;
What are they in your sicht, O Lord,
That ye should care for them?

A little lower than the angels
Ye made him at his birth,
Yet still to hae dominion
Owre a'thing on the earth:

Wi glory and wi honour crowned,
To rule aa flocks and herds,
Aa things in forest, hill and glen,
Beasts o' the field and birds,

Fish o' the sea and sweemin things,
Aa craiturs that draw breath.
O Lord our God, how excellent
Your name in aa the earth!

Praise ye the Lord

Praise ye the Lord, ye angels,
Praise him in heaven's height;
Praise ye the Lord, ye heavenly hosts,
Sun, moon and stars of light.

Praise him, ye heavens of heavens,
Created by his word;
Praise ye his name forever,
The everlasting Lord.

Praise ye his name from earth,
Sea creatures and all deeps;
Fire, hail and snow and vapour,
Storm winds and mountain steeps.

Praise ye his name, ye cedars,
All trees upon the earth;
All birds and beasts and creeping things;
Praise ye his matchless worth.

Kings of the earth, all nations;
Ye judges and old men;
Young men and maids, all children;
Praise ye the Lord again.

His name alone is excellent,
Praise ye his name abroad;
Above the heavens his glory shines,
The everlasting God.

To whom then will ye liken God?

Wha has measured the oceans
In the cup o' his haun,
And marked aff the heavens
Wi the breadth o' his span?

Wha has weighed in a balance
The primordial hills,
And measured the mountains
In the tilt o' his scales?

And wha has directed
The Spirit o' God?
Wha taught him his judgement?
Wha showed him the road?

The populous nations
As a drap in a pail,
Their uncoonted millions
As dust in his scales.

The islands as pebbles
Awash in the sea;
Aa nations as naething
Afore him shall be.

To whom then will ye liken God?
What image can ye mak?
Can gold and silver mak a God?
Or wood that winna brak?

Did ye nae ken? Have ye nae heard?
The Lord God sits enthroned
Abeen the circles o' the world
Since first the earth was formed.

He streetches oot earth's canopy,
The starry vault o' heaven,
And spreads it oot jist like a tent,
A dwellin-place to live in.

The princes and the rulers
He withers wi his breath;
Like chaff afore the whirlwind
They are scattered owre the earth.

"To whom then will ye liken me?
My equal, wha is he?"
Wha made the heavens, sun, moon and stars?
Lift up your eyes and see.

He calls the stars, each by its name,
He calls on them to rise
And licht the shinin vault o' heaven,
The people o' the skies.

O Israel, why do ye say,
"The Lord regards me not;
My way from God is hidden,
My cause by him forgot"?

Did ye nae ken? Have ye nae heard?
The Lord God faileth never;
Creator o' the universe,
His reign will laist forever.

And wha can search his wisdom?
His knowledge comprehend?
He gies the helpless power,
Revives the faint again.

The vera youths growe weary,
Aye, even the young men;
But they that wait upon the Lord
Renew their strength again.

They shall soar with wings as eagles,
High in the firmament;
They shall run and not be weary;
They shall walk and not be faint.

Solomon's Song

Rise up, my love, my fair one,
And come awa wi me.
The winter rains are ower,
The blossom's on the tree;

The flooers appear owre aa the earth;
The birds brak into sang,
The murmur o' the turtle dove
Is heard throughout the land;

The tender vines are fragrant,
The fig is on the tree.
Arise, my love, my fair one,
And come awa wi me.

for Elizabeth

I shall lead ye forth in Joyfulness

Seek ye the Lord when he is near,
While yet he may be socht:
Let the wicked man forsake his wyes,
And the evil man his thochts.

The Lord will freely pardon
If he but turn to him,
For God is great in mercy
And will forgie his sin.

"My thochts are nae your thochts," says God,
"And my wyes nae your wyes.
As the heavens are higher than the earth,
So higher far am I.

"As rain comes doon, and snaw fae heaven,
And watters aa the earth,
And gars it bloom and flourish,
So shall my word gang forth.

"It shall not fail in what I will
And void return to me,
But shall accomplish my desire,
My purpose, my decree.

"I shall lead ye forth in joyfulness
And peace, whare'er ye gang:
The mountains and the hills shall sing,
The trees shall clap their hauns."

The Heavens declare God's Glory

The heavens declare God's glory;
The skies his work proclaim;
Day unto day, and nicht to nicht,
His wisdom and his fame.

To every speech and language
Their message has gaen forth;
Their words oot to the world's end,
Their voice to aa the earth.

In the heavens has he set
The pavilion o' the sun.
Like a bridegroom to his mairrage,
In glory daes he come.

He rejoices and is glad
Like a strong man in a race,
As he strides across the heavens,
Naething hidden fae his face.

The law of God is perfect,
The weary soul revives.
His word is sure and steadfast;
It makes the simple wise.

"The teachin o' the Lord is richt,"
The joyful hert replies;
And radiant his commandments,
Enlightenin the eyes.

The fear o' God endureth
Forever, and is pure;
And altogether righteous
His judgements true and sure.

As sun ootshines the purest gold,
So they ootshine the sun;
And sweeter far than honey,
Than honey fae the comb.

And precious to his servant
The judgements o' the Lord;
By them is he instructed,
And great is his reward.

My life is but a little span

My life is but a little span,
Nae mair than a breath.
A movin shadow is this man;
Brief day, frail best, and death.

Lord, hear my prayer; I ken thee not,
A wanderer am I.
Forgie my sins, renew my strength,
O Lord, afore I die.

Too Wonderful

Three things there are too wonderful,
Aye, four I dinna ken:
An eagle's wye upon the wind;
A serpent's on a stane;

A man's wye wi a lassie;
A ship's wye throwe the sea.
Four things there are I dinna ken,
Too wonderful for me.

The Glory of God's Creation

Fae the darkness o' the whirlwind
God made his answer plain:
"Wha is this that darkens counsel
Speakin things he disna ken?

"Come, quit ye like a man, O Job,
And listen now to me;
And answer if ye ken, O Job,
What I will speir at thee.

"Whar were ye when I made the earth
And laid its cornerstane?
Wha measured oot its bounds, O Job?
Come, tell me if ye ken;

"When the mornin stars cam forth
And sang in harmony,
And aa the sons o' God
That shouted oot for glee.

"Wha shut up the sea wi doors
When it broke forth fae the womb,
And I made the clouds its garment,
Dark clouds and thickest gloom?

"I fixed its bounds and limits
And set its doors in place:
Here shall ye come, nae further,
And here your prood waves cease!

"Did you call forth the mornin, Job,
Or show the dawn its place?
Have ye seen the fountains o' the deep,
Or walked in the abyss?

"Have the gates o' death been shown to you,
The vera gates o' hell?
Have ye seen earth's vast expanses,
And measured them yoursel?

"Can ye trace the splendid paths o' licht?
And whar daes darkness hide?
Can ye tak them to their places?
Div you ken whar they bide?

"Have ye seen the treasures o' the snaw,
Or the storehoose o' the hail?
My weapons for the time o' war;
I fling them on the gale.

"Wha maks the storms and thunder
That brings the livin rain
To soak a parched and desert land,
And gars it bloom again?

"Div the dewdrops hae a father,
The hoarfrost and the rain?
Wha binds the winter seas wi ice,
Their watters hard as stane?

"Can ye bind the spangled Pleiades,
Or call oot Mazzaroth?
Can ye loose Orion's bands,
Or bring Arcturus forth?

"Div ye ken the laws o' heaven?
Can ye issue God's decree?
Can ye ask the clouds for watter?
Or gar the lichtnin flee?

"When the lion cubs are hungry
And the ravens cry for maet,
Wha feeds them in the desert
And brings them prey to aet?

"The deer that roam the mountains,
The wild goats on the scree,
Ken you their paths and birthplace?
Wha set the wild ass free?

"Gave you the war-horse strength, O Job,
And thunder in his mane?
He paws the grun and snorts the air,
His een like coals o' flame.

"He charges to the battle
And lauchs at death and fear;
The quiver rattles at his side,
The shield and glitterin spear.

"He lifts his noble heid and smells
The battle fae afar.
He lauchs to hear the trumpet-blast,
The shouts and noise o' war.

"The eagle seeks the mountain crag
And builds her nest on high;
She mounts and soars into the sun:
Can you direct her wye?"

Then Job made God his answer:
"Naething, Lord, is hid fae thee.
I hae spoken withoot knowledge,
Things too wonderful for me.

"Fae far awa I heard ye, Lord,
But now my een hae seen
Your glory, I despise mysel,
And repent o' what I've deen."

They that go down to the Sea in Ships

The men that sail the muckle seas
In ships to ply their trade;
They see God's wonders in the deep,
The works that he has made.

The tempest rises at his word,
The waves are lifted high;
The ship slides doon the endless troch,
Syne rears up to the sky.

Like drunken men the sailors reel;
They stagger back and fore.
Their vera souls are terrified,
Cowed by the tempest's roar.

They cry to God in their distress;
He hears their frenzied plea,
And calms the howlin tempest
And stills the ragin sea.

The wind is but a whisper;
The gentle sea is still.
He guides them safe to haven
Aneth the purple hill.

On the Wings of the Morning

O Lord, ye hae searched me and kent me.
Ye ken when I sit and I rise.
Ye ken aa my comins and goins;
Ye ken aa my thochts and my wyes.

Ye ken every word that I utter;
Ye beset me afore and ahin.
Such things are too wondrous for me, Lord;
Such heichts I can never attain.

And whar shall I gang fae your Spirit?
Or whar shall I flee fae yoursel?
If I mount up to heaven, ye're there,
And there in the black pits o' hell.

If I flee on the wings o' the mornin
To the uttermost pairts o' the sea,
Even there will your haun guide and keep me,
And the dark shall be licht aboot me.

He sends Springs doon the Valleys

He sends springs doon the valleys
That run among the hills.
Wild craiturs come to quench their thirst;
The wild ass drinks his fill.

The birds nest in the bonny trees
Along the windin stream,
And aa day lang they poor their sang
Among the branches green.

The earth is wi his goodness blessed;
He gars the sweet herbs growe,
That sheep and kye may aet their fill
Doon in the grassy howe.

God ripes the ear upon the wheat,
The grape upon the vine,
To gie man breid for sustenance
And cheer his hert wi wine.

God's trees drink deep o' moisture
And streetch up to the sun;
The birds nest in their branches,
Cedars o' Lebanon.

The stork nests in the fir tree;
The high hills are for goats;
The conies mak their hooses
Doon in among the rocks.

The moon marks aff the seasons;
The sun shines clear and bricht.
He kens his time o' settin;
He sinks, then comes the nicht.

The wild beasts o' the forest prowl;
The lions roar for prey.
God feeds them and they slink awa
Afore the brak o' day.

And aa day lang man daes his work
Until the West is reed.
God wraps him safe in slumber's shawl
When he lays doon his heid.

The vast and teemin oceans crawl
Wi craiturs, great and sma.
He kens their coontless multitudes
And feeds them, ane and aa.

O Lord, how wonderful your works,
Your mony gifts to man.
The earth is wi your goodness filled
And cradled in your haun.

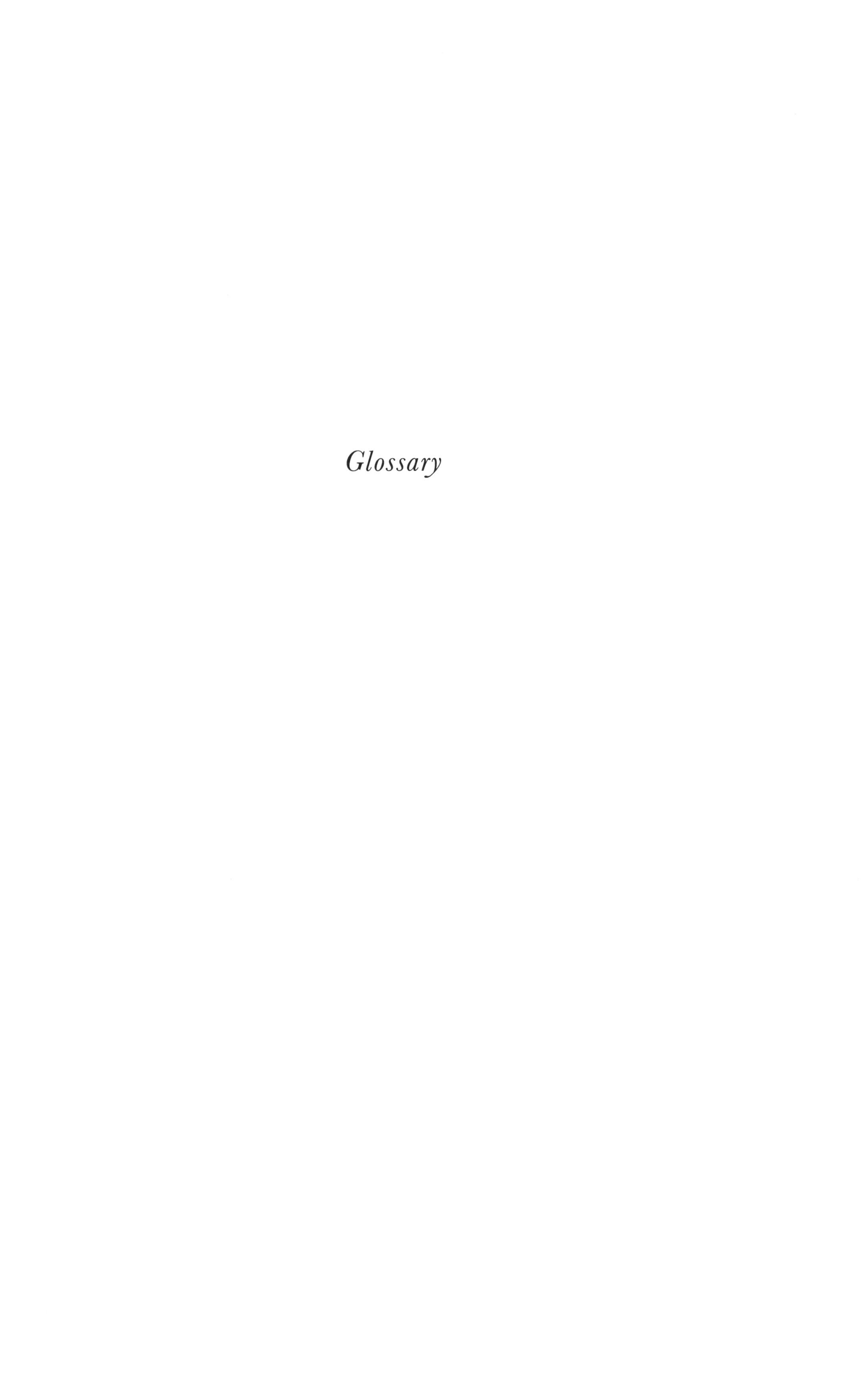

Glossary

Choice of words

Most Scots words have many regional variants, so it is impossible to please all of the people all of the time, as any variant will seem *wrong* to someone.

The language of the poems is based on the vernacular of the North-east, but I have tried not to use too many local words, preferring generally-known variants where these existed, and the stories should be accessible to any Scot or interested reader.

In choosing words, the flow of the verse and clarity of expression have taken precedence over 'authentic' dialect, and I have not hestitated to use English words where these suited my purpose better.

Verbs

Predictable past participles are not listed, e.g. '-it' and '-in' endings. So 'chap' — to chop — is listed, but not 'chappit' — chopped. 'Difficult' or unpredictable past participles are listed, e.g. 'gaun' — going.

'-in' endings

Where the only difference between an English word and its Scots form is the '-in' ending instead of '-ing', the word is not listed, e.g. 'mornin'.

'-ie' endings

The suffix '-ie' is used for the diminutive, as in 'lounie' — small boy. It may sometimes have familiar or affectionate connotations, e.g. in 'bairnie'.

English words

Certain English words which may not be well-known, e.g. 'coney' and 'gunnel', are included for convenience.

A

a', aa — all
abeen — above
aboord — aboard
aboot — about
adee — wrong (*in 'what's adee?'*)
ae — one
aet — to eat
aff — off
afore — before
ahin — behind
aifter — after
ain — own
airms — arms
ana' — as well
ane — one
aneth — beneath
anither — another
a'richt — alright
aroon — around
aside — beside
a'thing — everything
atween — between
auld — old
aulder, auler — older
auldest — eldest
ava — of all; at all
awa — away

B

back and fore — to and fro
bad — bid
bade — stayed
bairn — a child
baith — both
banes — bones
banshee — a female spirit whose wail was thought to presage death (Gael. *ban-sith* a fairy woman)
befa — befall
beset — to enfold
bide — to stay; to live (reside)
blaw — to blow; to blossom
bleed — blood
bleed-reed — blood-red
blin — blind
bocht — bought
bonny — beautiful, excellent; beautifully
brae — a hillside; a steep slope
brak — to break
brak o' sky — daybreak
breid — bread
bricht — bright
brither — brother
brocht — brought
burn — a stream

C

ca' — to call
cam — came
canna — can't
caul, cauld — cold
chap — to chop
chauve — to struggle; to work laboriously
clim — to climb
coney — the rock hyrax
coo — a cow
coont — to count
coontless — countless
couldna — couldn't
cra — a crow
craitur — creature (*sympathetic or affectionate*)
cry — to call

D

dae — do
daes — does
daylicht — daylight
dee — to do; to die
deein — doing
deed — died

deen .... done; finished
deid .... dead
didna .... didn't
dinna .... don't
disna .... doesn't
div .... do (*emphatic & interrogative*)
doo .... a pigeon
doon .... down
dooncast .... downcast
doonfa .... downfall
drap .... a drop
droon .... to drown

E

'ear .... a year
een .... eyes
eeseless .... useless
evermair .... evermore

F

fa' .... to fall
fae .... from
faimly .... family
fash .... to vex (*oneself*)
fecht .... a fight; to fight
fechtin .... fighting
feel .... a fool
fell .... evil
fit .... a foot
flee .... a fly; to fly; to flee
fleer .... a floor
flooer .... a flower
focht .... fought
fooner .... to founder
forgie .... to forgive
fortnicht .... a fortnight

G

gaed .... went
gaen .... gone
gairden .... a garden
gaither .... to gather
gang .... to go
gar .... to make (*a person or thing do something*)
gaun .... going
gie .... to give
gien .... given
gled .... glad
good-dother .... daughter-in-law
greet .... to weep
growe .... to grow
grun .... ground
gunnels .... the rails of a ship
g'wa .... go away (*abbr. of 'gang awa'*)

H

hadna .... hadn't
hae .... to have
hale .... whole; healthy
hale jing-bang .... a considerable number
hame .... home
haud .... to hold
haud your wisht .... hold your tongue
haun .... hand
havena .... haven't
heicht .... height
heid .... head
hersel .... herself
hert .... heart
hetter .... hotter
himsel .... himself
hoose .... a house
horny gollach .... the earwig
howe .... hollow

I

ill .... evil
ither .... other
itsel .... itself

J

jile .... jail
jine .... to join

hale jing-bang .... a considerable number
jist .... just

K

ken .... to know
kent .... knew
kittlin...................... a kitten
kye .... cattle

L

laist .... to last
lang .... long
lang syne.................. long since
langer .... longer
lassie .... a girl; daughter
lauch .... to laugh
lauchter.................... laughter
licht .... light
lichtnin .... lightning
lichtsome .... light-hearted
the lift .... the heavens
lintie .... the linnet
loun .... a boy, youth; son
lounie .... a small boy
loup .... to leap
lour .... to look dark and threatening

M

maet........................ food
mair .... more
mairriage .... marriage
maist .... most
maister .... master
mak .... to make
maun .... must
mavis .... the song thrush
micht .... might
mind .... to remember
mither .... mother
mony .... many
moose .... a mouse
muckle..................... enormous, great, huge, mighty
mysel .... myself

N

nae .... no, not
naebody.................... no-one
naething .... nothing
naewye .... nowhere
nicht........................ night
noo .... now

O

o'........................... of
ony .... any
onywye .... anyway
oor .... our
oot .... out
ootshine .... outshine
ootside.................... outside
or .... before
orra .... disreputable
ower, owre .... over

P

pairt....................... part
park .... a field
peer .... poor
pey .... to pay
pint....................... to point
pit........................ to put
poor .... to pour
prood.................... proud
puddock .... a frog

Q

quaet .... quiet
quine .... a girl
quit...................... to bear (*oneself*)

R

reed .... red
reek .... smoke
richt .... right
roon .... round
rowth .... profusion

S

sae .... so
saftly .... softly
sair .... hard, laborious, sorely
sang .... a song
seen .... soon
seener .... sooner
shieling .... a high summer pasture
sic .... such
sicht .... sight
sleekit .... cunning
sma .... small
snaw .... snow
socht .... sought
sodjer .... a soldier
sparra .... a sparrow
speir .... to ask
stane .... stone
staun .... to stand
steen .... stone
steeny .... stony
steer .... to stir
stowe .... to stow
streetch .... to stretch
sweem .... to swim
syne .... then
lang syne .... long since

T

ta'en .... taken
tak .... to take
tap .... top
telt .... told
thegither .... together
thocht .... thought
thoosan .... a thousand
threid .... thread
throwe .... through
ticht .... tight
till .... to
timmers .... timbers
toun .... a town
traivel .... to travel
traiveller .... a traveller
troch .... a trough
twa .... two

U

uncoonted .... uncounted
unkent .... unknown

V

vera .... very
vratch .... wretch

W

wa' .... a wall
warsle .... to struggle
wasna .... wasn't
watter .... water
watterticht .... watertight
wauken .... to wake
wee bit .... tiny
weel .... well
weemen .... women
weemenfolk .... womenfolk
weer .... to wear
weet .... wet
weicht .... weight
wha .... who
whaal .... a whale
whaever .... whoever
whar .... where
whare'er .... wherever
whiles .... sometimes
wi .... with
win .... to reach (*a place*) despite difficultie

winda...................... a window
winna...................... won't
winner..................... to wonder
wir .... our (*unstressed*)
wisht .... be quiet
haud your wisht .... hold your tongue
withoot .... without
wouldna .... wouldn't
wye......................... way

Y

ye .... you
yon......................... that
yoursel .... yourself
yowe....................... a ewe

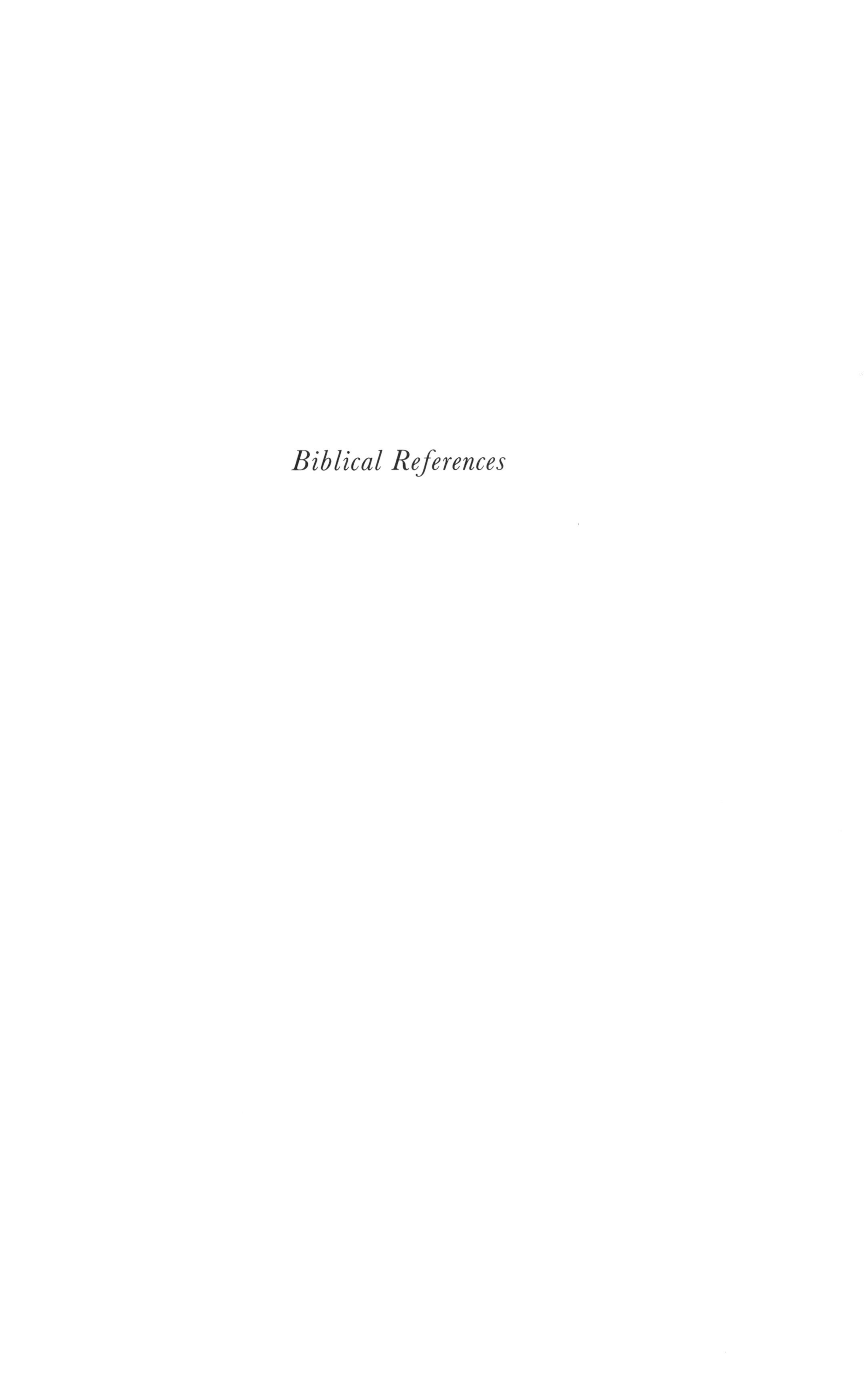

Biblical References

Old Testament Tales

Psalms, Prayers and Promises